SH*T
TRUMP
SAYS

**Flips, Flops, Flattery, and Falsehoods
from Our 45th President**

Castle Point Publishing
www.castlepointpub.com

ISBN: 978-0-9982297-4-4
Manufactured in Slovenia
10 9 8 7 6 5 4 3 2 1

DOGS, FAKE NEWS, AND OTHER ENEMIES OF THE PEOPLE

HAPPY NEW YEAR TO EVERYONE, INCLUDING THE HATERS AND THE FAKE NEWS MEDIA! 2019 WILL BE A FANTASTIC YEAR FOR THOSE NOT SUFFERING FROM TRUMP DERANGEMENT SYNDROME. JUST CALM DOWN AND ENJOY THE RIDE, GREAT THINGS ARE HAPPENING FOR OUR COUNTRY!

Twitter, January 1, 2019

Joe Biden got tongue-tied over the weekend when he was unable to properly deliver a very simple line about his decision to run for President. Get used to it, **ANOTHER LOW I.Q. INDIVIDUAL!**

Twitter, March 18, 2019

I HEARD POORLY RATED @MORNING_JOE SPEAKS BADLY OF ME (DON'T WATCH ANYMORE). THEN HOW COME LOW I.Q. CRAZY MIKA, ALONG WITH PSYCHO JOE, CAME...

Twitter, June 29, 2017

...TO MAR-A-LAGO
3 NIGHTS IN A ROW
AROUND NEW YEAR'S
EVE, AND INSISTED
ON JOINING ME. SHE
WAS BLEEDING BADLY
FROM A FACE-LIFT.
I SAID NO!

Twitter, June 29, 2017

Ted Cruz lifts the Bible high into the air and then lies like a dog—over and over again! The Evangelicals in S.C. figured him out & said no!

Twitter, February 23, 2016

LeBron James was just interviewed by the dumbest man on television, Don Lemon. He made Lebron look smart, which isn't easy to do. I like Mike!

Twitter, August 3, 2018

YOU'RE DISGUSTING.

To opposing counsel upon her request for a
breast-pump break during court proceedings,
The New York Times, July 28, 2015

When you give a crazed, crying LOWLIFE a break, and give her a job at the White House, I guess it just didn't work out. Good work by General Kelly for quickly firing that DOG!

Twitter, regarding Omarosa Manigault-Newman, reality star and director of communications in the White House's Office of Public Liaison, August 14, 2018

FACEBOOK, GOOGLE AND TWITTER,
NOT TO MENTION THE CORRUPT
MEDIA, ARE SOOO ON THE SIDE OF
THE RADICAL LEFT DEMOCRATS.
BUT FEAR NOT, WE WILL WIN
ANYWAY, JUST LIKE WE DID
BEFORE! #MAGA

Twitter, March 19, 2019

While the press doesn't like writing about it, nor do I need them to, **I donate** my yearly Presidential salary of **$400,000.00** to different agencies throughout the year, this to **Homeland Security.** If I didn't do it there would be hell to pay from the **FAKE NEWS MEDIA!**

Twitter, March 18, 2019

@BrentBozell, one of the National Review lightweights, came to my office begging for money like a dog. Why doesn't he say that?

Twitter, January 22, 2016

THE FAKE NEWS MEDIA IS GOING CRAZY! THEY ARE TOTALLY UNHINGED AND IN MANY WAYS, AFTER WITNESSING FIRST HAND THE DAMAGE THEY DO TO SO MANY INNOCENT AND DECENT PEOPLE, I ENJOY WATCHING. IN 7 YEARS, WHEN I AM NO LONGER IN OFFICE, THEIR RATINGS WILL DRY UP AND THEY WILL BE GONE!

Twitter, July 31, 2018

I believe it will be **CRAZY BERNIE SANDERS** vs. **SLEEPY JOE BIDEN** as the two finalists to run against maybe the best Economy in the history of our Country [and MANY other great things]! I look forward to facing whoever it may be. **MAY GOD REST THEIR SOUL!**

Twitter, April 16, 2019

Crazy Joe Biden is trying to act like a tough guy. Actually, he is weak, both mentally and physically, and yet he threatens me, for the second time, with physical assault. He doesn't know me, but he would go down fast and hard, crying all the way. DON'T THREATEN PEOPLE JOE!

Twitter, March 22, 2018

If Abe Lincoln came back to life, he would lose New York and he would lose California.

Interview with
The Associated Press,
April 23, 2017

Crooked Hillary Clinton
is the worst [and biggest]
loser of all time. She
just can't stop, which
is so good for the
Republican Party. Hillary,
get on with your life
and give it another try
in three years!

Twitter, November 18, 2017

OBABA IS OUR UNLUCKY PRESIDENT. EVERYTHING HE TOUCHES TURNS INTO A MESS. SOME PEOPLE JUST DON'T HAVE IT!

Twitter, September 17, 2012

Wow was Ted Cruz disloyal to his very capable director of communication.
He used him as a scape-goat—fired like a dog! Ted panicked.

Twitter, February 23, 2016

Bob Iger of ABC called Valerie Jarrett to let her know that "ABC does not tolerate comments like those" made by Roseanne Barr. Gee, he never called President Donald J. Trump to apologize for the HORRIBLE statements made and said about me on ABC. Maybe I just didn't get the call?

Twitter, May 30, 2018

So it was indeed [just proven in court papers] "last in his class" [Annapolis] John McCain that sent the Fake Dossier to the FBI and Media hoping to have it printed BEFORE the Election. He & the Dems, working together, failed [as usual]. Even the Fake News refused this garbage!

Twitter, March 17, 2019

If CROOKED HILLARY would have won this election, and if she came here, which is about a zero percent chance after the election, SHE'D HAVE 200 PEOPLE IN A CONFERENCE ROOM IN A SMALL HOTEL.

Remarks about Hillary Clinton's
would-be crowd numbers,
campaign rally,
North Dakota, June 27, 2018

He's a *jealous fool* and not a bright person. He's good looking. Other than that, *he's got nothing.*

On Mitt Romney in an interview with
The New York Times, March 18, 2016

It's truly incredible that shows like Saturday Night Live, **NOT FUNNY/NO TALENT,** can spend all of their time knocking the same person (me), over & over, without so much of a mention of **"THE OTHER SIDE."** Like an advertisement without consequences. Same with Late Night Shows...

Twitter, March 17, 2019

He's like a lost soul, Jeb Bush . . . this poor, pathetic, low-energy guy.

Video from *The Washington Post*,
January 21, 2016

Congresswoman Maxine Waters, an extraordinarily low IQ person, has become, together with Nancy Pelosi, the Face of the Democrat Party. She has just called for harm to supporters, of which there are many, of the Make America Great Again movement. Be careful what you wish for Max!

Twitter, June 25, 2018

She gets out and she starts asking me all sorts of ridiculous questions. You could see there was blood coming out of her eyes.

Blood coming out of her wherever.

Interview with CNN,
in reference to journalist Megyn Kelly,
August 8, 2015

WELCOME TO THE RACE SLEEPY JOE. I ONLY HOPE YOU HAVE THE INTELLIGENCE, LONG IN DOUBT, TO WAGE A SUCCESSFUL PRIMARY CAMPAIGN. IT WILL BE NASTY— YOU WILL BE DEALING WITH PEOPLE WHO TRULY HAVE SOME VERY SICK & DEMENTED IDEAS. BUT IF YOU MAKE IT, I WILL SEE YOU AT THE STARTING GATE!

Twitter, in reference to Joe Biden, April 25, 2019

A VERY
STABLE
GENIUS

I want to thank the **WHITE HOUSE** Historical Association and all of the people that work so hard with Melania, with everybody, to keep this incredible house or building, or **WHATEVER YOU WANT TO CALL IT** — because there really is no name for it; it is special — and we keep it in tip-top shape. We call it sometimes **TIPPY-TOP SHAPE.** And it's a great, great place.

Describing the White House,
White House Easter Egg Roll, April 2, 2018

*You know, I know the smart people. **I really know the smart people.** I deal with the smart people.*

Interview with *Larry King Live*,
CNN, October 8, 1999

AFTER HAVING WRITTEN MANY BEST-SELLING BOOKS, AND SOMEWHAT PRIDING MYSELF ON MY ABILITY TO WRITE, IT SHOULD BE NOTED THAT THE FAKE NEWS CONSTANTLY LIKES TO PORE OVER MY TWEETS LOOKING FOR A MISTAKE. I CAPITALIZE CERTAIN WORDS ONLY FOR EMPHASIS, NOT B/C THEY SHOULD BE CAPITALIZED!

Twitter, July 3, 2018

It's like in golf... A lot of people—
I don't want this to sound trivial—
but a lot of people are switching
to these really long putters, very
unattractive... **IT'S WEIRD.** You
see these great players with these
really long putters, because they
can't sink three-footers anymore.
And, **I HATE IT.** I am a
traditionalist. I have so many
fabulous friends who happen to
be gay, but I am a traditionalist.

Interview with *The New York Times*,
regarding his stance on gay marriage,
May 1, 2011

THESE PEOPLE. WE GOT A BUNCHA REAL DUMMIES, I'LL TELL YA.

Video from *The Washington Post*,
January 21, 2016

I loved my previous life. I had so many things going. **This is more work than in my previous life.** I thought it would be easier.

Interview with Reuters
regarding the presidency,
April 27, 2017

Nobody knew health care could be so complicated.

Governors' meeting
at the White House,
February 27, 2017

HE'S NOT LYIN' TED ANYMORE. HE'S BEAUTIFUL TED. I CALL HIM TEXAS TED.

Campaign rally for Ted Cruz, Houston, Texas, October 22, 2018

RIGHT NOW, IN A NUMBER OF STATES, THE LAWS ALLOW A BABY TO BE **BORN** FROM HIS OR HER MOTHER'S WOMB IN THE NINTH MONTH. **IT IS WRONG;** IT HAS TO CHANGE.

Remarks to March for Life
participants and pro-life leaders,
January 19, 2018

You are somewhat more traditional politicians (than me).

Immigration talk-a-thon,
January 9, 2018

I said, **"Oh, I am so smart. I am the smartest person."** My uncle was a great professor at MIT for forty years. Can you believe? Forty years. I said, **"But I'm smarter than him. I'm smarter than anybody."**

Campaign rally, North Dakota,
June 27, 2018

You have somebody else that sits and reads and thinks, and I'm a thinker and I have been a thinker, and perhaps people don't think of me that way, because you don't see me in that forum. But I am a thinker... I'm a very deep thinker. I know what's happening.

News conference,
Palm Beach, Florida,
March 11, 2016

...Actually, throughout my life, my two greatest assets have been mental stability and being, like, really smart. Crooked Hillary Clinton also played these cards very hard and, as everyone knows, went down in flames. I went from VERY successful businessman, to top T.V. Star...

Twitter, January 6, 2018

...to President of the United States (on my first try). I think that would qualify as not smart, but genius... and a very stable genius at that!

Twitter, January 6, 2018

"The best thing ever to happen to Twitter is Donald Trump." @MariaBartiromo So true, but they don't treat me well as a Republican. Very discriminatory, hard for people to sign on. Constantly taking people off list. Big complaints from many people. Different names—over 100 M...

Twitter, April 23, 2019

...BUT SHOULD BE MUCH HIGHER THAN THAT IF TWITTER WASN'T PLAYING THEIR POLITICAL GAMES. NO WONDER CONGRESS WANTS TO GET INVOLVED —AND THEY SHOULD. MUST BE MORE, AND FAIRER, COMPANIES TO GET OUT THE WORD!

Twitter, April 23, 2019

I WOULD SAY COMMUNICATION WOULD BE A LITTLE BIT LESS THAN AN A BECAUSE I DON'T THINK WE'VE GOTTEN THE WORD OUT WHAT WE'VE DONE BECAUSE I THINK WE'RE SO BUSY GETTING IT DONE THAT WE'RE NOT TALKING ABOUT IT.

Interview with
The Washington Examiner,
April 28, 2017

I have learned
much more from
conducting my own
random surveys
than I could have
ever learned from
the greatest
consulting firms.

Trump: The Art of the Deal, 1987

We appreciate it very much, Tim Apple.

Speaking to Apple CEO Tim Cook,
March 6, 2019

WINNERS WHO ALWAYS WIN

Will someone from his depleted and food-starved regime please inform him that I too have a Nuclear Button, but it is a much bigger & more powerful one than his, and my Button works!

Twitter, in reference to
Supreme Leader of North Korea
Kim Jong-un's nuclear weapons,
January 2, 2018

I will never change this hairstyle, I like it. It fits my head. Those who criticize me are only losers and envy people. And it is not a wig, it's my hair. Do you want to touch it?

Interview with *Veja*, February 18, 2014

I THINK WE'VE DONE MORE THAN PERHAPS ANY PRESIDENT IN THE FIRST 100 DAYS.

Interview with
The Washington Examiner,
April 28, 2017

I'm really rich.

2016 presidential campaign announcement, New York, June 16, 2015

OF COURSE WE SHOULD HAVE CAPTURED OSAMA BIN LADEN LONG BEFORE WE DID. I POINTED HIM OUT IN MY BOOK JUST BEFORE THE ATTACK ON THE WORLD TRADE CENTER. PRESIDENT CLINTON FAMOUSLY MISSED HIS SHOT. WE PAID PAKISTAN BILLIONS OF DOLLARS & THEY NEVER TOLD US HE WAS LIVING THERE. FOOLS!

Twitter, November 19, 2018

As a kid, I was making a building with blocks in our playroom. I didn't have enough. So I asked my younger brother Robert if I could borrow some of his. He said, "Okay, but you have to give them back when you're done." I used all of my blocks, then all of his blocks, and when I was done I had a great building, which I then glued together. **Robert never did get those blocks back.**

Interview with *Esquire*,
January 2004

And I wish those cameras would circle the room to see how many thousands of people are here, because, you know, on the screen I look—and all you see are those few beautiful, wonderful people—I don't know who the hell I—but you've got a nice group over there. I know you have Mike and some others. They're going to be so famous.

Campaign rally,
North Dakota,
June 27, 2018

...TO THE PEOPLE THAT GOT YOU THERE. KEEP FIGHTING FOR TUCKER, AND FIGHT HARD FOR @JUDGEJEANINE. **YOUR COMPETITORS ARE JEALOUS**—THEY ALL WANT WHAT YOU'VE GOT—NUMBER ONE. DON'T HAND IT TO THEM ON A SILVER PLATTER. THEY CAN'T BEAT YOU, YOU CAN ONLY BEAT YOURSELVES!

Twitter, March 17, 2019

[Kim Jong-un] speaks and his people sit up at attention. **I WANT my people to do the same.**

Interview with
Fox & Friends,
June 15, 2018

If you took a poll in the FBI, **I WOULD WIN THAT POLL** more than anyone has ever won a poll.

Interview with
Fox & Friends,
June 15, 2018

I think my positions are going to be what the people in this room come up with.

Immigration talk-a-thon,
January 9, 2018

I say, **NOT IN A BRAGGADOCIOS WAY,** I've made billions and billions of dollars dealing with people all around the world.

CNN Republican debate,
September 16, 2015

I **WIN**, I ALWAYS **WIN**. IN THE END **I ALWAYS WIN**, WHETHER IT'S IN GOLF, WHETHER IT'S IN TENNIS, WHETHER IT'S IN LIFE, **I JUST ALWAYS WIN**. AND I TELL PEOPLE **I ALWAYS WIN**, BECAUSE I DO.

TrumpNation:
The Art of Being The Donald,
2005

I would give myself an A+.

Interview with *Fox & Friends*,
April 27, 2018

IT'S AMAZING HOW OFTEN I AM RIGHT.

Twitter, March 24, 2016

I was hundreds of millions in debt and beat bankruptcy twice—so what?

Remarks in *The Daily Mail*,
October 30, 2010

I've known Paris Hilton from the time she's 12, her parents are friends of mine, and the first time I saw her she walked into the room and I said, "Who the hell is that?" **At 12, I wasn't interested . . . but she was beautiful.**

Interview with *The Howard Stern Show*, 2003

You'll find that when you become very successful, the people that you will like best are the people that are less successful than you, because when you go to a table you can tell them all of these wonderful stories, and they'll sit back and listen. Does that make sense to you? Always be around unsuccessful people because everybody will respect you.

Campaign rally,
De Pere, Wisconsin,
March 30, 2016

I am the world's greatest person.

Phone conversation with Australian
Prime Minister Malcolm Turnbull,
January 27, 2017

When a country (USA)
is losing many billions of
dollars on trade with
virtually every country it
does business with, trade
wars are good, and easy
to win. Example, when we
are down $100 billion
with a certain country and
they get cute, don't trade
anymore—we win big.
It's easy!

Twitter, March 2, 2018

I meet these people. They call them the elite! These people. I look at them, I say, that's elite? WE GOT MORE MONEY. WE GOT MORE BRAINS. WE GOT BETTER HOUSES, APARTMENTS. WE GOT NICER BOATS. We are smarter than they are and they say "the elite." WE ARE THE ELITE.

Campaign rally, North Dakota,
June 27, 2018

Lowest-rated Oscars in HISTORY. Problem is, WE DON'T HAVE STARS ANYMORE—EXCEPT YOUR PRESIDENT (just kidding, of course)!

Twitter, March 6, 2018

So horrible to watch the massive fire at Notre Dame Cathedral in Paris. Perhaps flying water tankers could be used to put it out. Must act quickly!

Twitter, April 15, 2019

Spoke to @TigerWoods to congratulate him on the great victory he had in yesterday's @TheMasters, & to inform him that because of his incredible Success & Comeback in Sports (Golf) and, more importantly, LIFE, I will be presenting him with the PRESIDENTIAL MEDAL OF FREEDOM!

Twitter, April 15, 2019

THANK YOU, WORKING HARD! 53% APPROVAL RATING.

Twitter, April 9, 2019

I'M ALSO HONORED TO HAVE THE GREATEST TEMPERAMENT THAT ANYBODY HAS.

Campaign rally,
Jacksonville, Florida,
November 3, 2016

And I'm very proud of it because you are very, very special people. That I can tell you. Thank you. Nice hat. Look at that beautiful hat.

Roundtable discussion on Tax Reform, White Sulphur Springs, West Virginia, April 5, 2018

CLIMATE CHANGE AND OTHER LIES

It's freezing
and snowing in
New York—

WE NEED
GLOBAL
WARMING!

Twitter, November 7, 2012

I'm going to be very restrained, if I use it at all, **I'm going to be very restrained.**

Interview with *60 Minutes*,
regarding his use of Twitter as president,
November 12, 2016

I just wanna thank all of the incredible men and women who have done such a great job in helping with Florence. This is a tough hurricane. One of the wettest we've ever seen from a standpoint of water.

Presidential video released on Twitter,
September 18, 2018

One of the problems that a lot of people like myself – we have very high levels of intelligence, but we're not necessarily such believers. You look at our air and our water, and it's right now at a record clean. But when you look at China and you look at parts of Asia and when you look at South America, and when you look at many other places in this world, including Russia, including – just many other places – the air is incredibly dirty. And when you're talking about an atmosphere, oceans are very small. And it blows over and it sails over. I mean, we take thousands of tons of garbage off our beaches all the time that comes over from Asia. It just flows right down the Pacific, it flows, and we say where does this come from. And it takes many people to start off with.

Interview with *The Washington Post*,
November 27, 2018

*Beautiful weather all over our great country, a perfect day for all Women to March. **Get out there now to celebrate the historic milestones and unprecedented economic success and wealth creation that has taken place over the last 12 months. Lowest female unemployment in 18 years!***

Twitter, January 20, 2018

I HAVE A GREAT RELATIONSHIP WITH AFRICAN AMERICANS, as you possibly have heard. I just have great respect for them. And they like me. **I LIKE THEM.**

Interview with
Anderson Cooper 360,
July 23, 2015

The new Fake News narrative is that there is CHAOS in the White House. Wrong! People will always come & go, and I want strong dialogue before making a final decision. I still have some people that I want to change [always seeking perfection]. There is no Chaos, only great Energy!

Twitter, March 6, 2018

BRUTAL AND
EXTENDED COLD
BLAST COULD SHATTER
ALL RECORDS –
WHATEVER HAPPENED
TO GLOBAL WARMING?

Twitter, November 21, 2018

I look very much forward to showing my financials, because they are **HUGE.**

Interview with *Time*,
April 14, 2011

It's really cold outside, they are calling it a major freeze, weeks ahead of normal.

MAN, WE COULD USE A BIG FAT DOSE OF GLOBAL WARMING!

Twitter, October 19, 2015

BUT YOU ALSO HAD PEOPLE THAT WERE VERY FINE PEOPLE ON BOTH SIDES.

To a reporter in reference to the participants of the deadly Charlottesville, Virginia, protest, August 15, 2017

*I will be phenomenal
to the women. I mean,
I want to help women.*

Interview with *Face the Nation*,
August 9, 2015

I AM A YOUNG, VIBRANT MAN.

To reporters outside
the White House, April 26, 2019

DIVERSITY, ILLEGALS, AND A GREAT BIG WALL

WE'RE ROUNDING 'EM UP
IN A VERY HUMANE WAY,
IN A VERY NICE WAY.
AND THEY'RE GOING TO BE
HAPPY BECAUSE THEY
WANT TO BE LEGALIZED.
AND, BY THE WAY, I KNOW
IT DOESN'T SOUND NICE.
BUT NOT EVERYTHING
IS NICE.

Interview with *60 Minutes*,
September 27, 2015

THE DEMOCRATS ARE TRYING TO BELITTLE THE CONCEPT OF A WALL, CALLING IT OLD FASHIONED. THE FACT IS THERE IS NOTHING ELSE'S THAT WILL WORK, AND THAT HAS BEEN TRUE FOR THOUSANDS OF YEARS. IT'S LIKE THE WHEEL, THERE IS NOTHING BETTER. I KNOW TECH BETTER THAN ANYONE,& TECHNOLOGY...

Twitter, December 21, 2018

The country is doing well in so many ways. But there's such divisiveness.

Immigration talk-a-thon,
January 9, 2018

THE U.S. CANNOT ALLOW EBOLA-INFECTED PEOPLE BACK. PEOPLE THAT GO TO FAR AWAY PLACES TO HELP OUT ARE GREAT—BUT MUST SUFFER THE CONSEQUENCES!

Twitter, September 2, 2014

The Wall is being built and is well under construction. Big impact will be made. Many additional contracts are close to being signed. Far ahead of schedule despite all of the Democrat Obstruction and Fake News!

Twitter, March 8, 2019

I AM A TARIFF MAN. When people or countries come in to raid the great wealth of our Nation, I want them to pay for the privilege of doing so. It will always be the best way to max out our economic power. We are right now taking in $billions in Tariffs. MAKE AMERICA RICH AGAIN

Twitter, December 4, 2018

When you see the other side chopping off heads, **waterboarding doesn't sound very severe.**

Interview with *This Week with George Stephanopoulos*, August 2, 2016

I think I could have stopped it because I have very tough illegal immigration policies, and people aren't coming into this country unless they're vetted and vetted properly.

On preventing the September 11th terrorist attacks in an interview with *Hannity*, October 20, 2015

Wouldn't you love to see one of these NFL owners, when somebody disrespects our flag, to say, "Get that son of a bitch off the field right now. Out! He's fired. He's fired!"

In reference to NFL players'
peaceful protests of kneeling
during the national anthem,
Huntsville, Alabama,
September 22, 2017

What I won't do is take in two hundred thousand Syrians who could be ISIS . . . I have been watching this migration. And I see the people. I mean, they're men. They're mostly men, and they're strong men. These are physically young, strong men. They look like prime-time soldiers. Now it's probably not true, but where are the women? So, you ask two things. Number one, why aren't they fighting for their country? And number two, I don't want these people coming over here.

Interview with *Face the Nation*,
November 10, 2015

Our country is in serious trouble. We don't have victories any more. We used to have victories but [now] we don't have them. **When was the last time anybody saw us beating, let's say, China, in a trade deal? They kill us. I beat China all the time. All the time.**

2016 presidential campaign announcement,
New York, June 16, 2015

The Wall is being rapidly built! **THE ECONOMY IS GREAT!** Our Country is Respected again!

Twitter, April 23, 2019

I AM PROUD TO SHUT DOWN THE GOVERNMENT FOR BORDER SECURITY.

Oval Office meeting with Chuck Schumer and Nancy Pelosi prior to the longest and most damaging government shutdown in United States history, December 21, 2018

Why are we having all
these people from
shithole countries
coming here?

White House meeting,
January 11, 2018

I DON'T PUT BORDERS ON MYSELF OR MY INTERESTS.

Remarks in *The Daily Mail*,
October 30, 2010

FLIP-FLOPS

I have no intention of running for president.

Interview with *Time* magazine,
September 14, 1987

I am officially running for president.

Candidacy announcement speech,
June 16, 2015

I don't want it for myself. I don't need it for myself.

Interview with *ABC News*,
November 20, 2015

I wanted to do this for myself. . . . I had to do it for myself.

Interview with *Time* magazine,
August 18, 2015

I'm not a POLITICIAN.

Interview with CNN,
August 11, 2015

I'm no different than a POLITICIAN running for office.

Interview with *The New York Times*,
July 28, 2015

I'm totally pro-choice.

Interview with *Fox News*,
October 31, 1999

I'm pro-life.

Speech at the Conservative
Political Action Conference,
February 10, 2011

Look, I'm very pro-choice.

Interview with *Meet the Press*,
October 24, 1999

I am very, very proud to say that I'm pro-life.

Republican presidential debate,
Cleveland, Ohio, August 6, 2015

IF I EVER RAN FOR OFFICE, I'D DO BETTER AS A DEMOCRAT THAN AS A REPUBLICAN—AND THAT'S NOT BECAUSE I'D BE MORE LIBERAL, BECAUSE I'M CONSERVATIVE.

Interview with *Playboy* magazine,
March 1990

I'M A REGISTERED REPUBLICAN. I'M A PRETTY CONSERVATIVE GUY. I'M SOMEWHAT LIBERAL ON SOCIAL ISSUES, ESPECIALLY HEALTH CARE, ETC.

Interview with *Larry King Live*, CNN,
October 8, 1999

If two people dig each other, they dig each other.

Blog post on Trump
University's *Trump Blog*,
December 22, 2005

I'm against gay marriage.

Interview with *Fox News*,
April 14, 2011

It's always good to do things nice and complicated so that nobody can figure it out.

Comment published in *The New Yorker*,
May 19, 1997

The simplest approach is often the most effective.

In *Trump: The Art of the Deal*, 1987

My attention span is short.

Trump: Surviving at the Top, 1990

I have an attention span that's as long as it has to be.

Interview with *Time*,
August 18, 2015

I do listen to people. I hire experts. I hire top, top people. And I do listen.

Republican presidential debate, Greenville,
South Carolina, February 13, 2016

My primary consultant is myself.

Interview with *Morning Joe*, MSNBC,
March 16, 2016

I surround myself with good people, and then I give myself the luxury of trusting them.

In *Trump: Surviving at the Top*, 1990

My motto is "Hire the best people, and don't trust them."

Trump: Think Big, 2009

Stay as close to home as possible. Travel is time-consuming and, in my opinion, boring.

Trump: Surviving at the Top, 1990

**There's no excuse
for staying home;
the world's
too fantastic
to miss out on it.
I wish I could
travel more.**

*Trump: Think Like a
Billionaire,* 2004

If you can avoid an altercation, do so.

Trump: Think Like a Billionaire, 2004

If someone attacks you, do not hesitate. Go for the jugular.

In *Trump: Think Big*, 2009

I think I've been a very good husband.

Interview with CNN, February 9, 2011

What the hell do I know, I've been divorced twice?

Trump: Think Big, 2007

I KNOW HILLARY AND I THINK SHE'D MAKE A GREAT PRESIDENT.

Blog post on Trump University's
Trump Blog, March 13, 2008

HILLARY WILL BE A DISASTER AS A PRESIDENT.

Interview with *NBC News*,
July 9, 2015

I'm not a hunter and don't approve of killing animals. I strongly disagree with my sons who are hunters.

Twitter, March 15, 2012

My sons love to hunt. They are members of the NRA, very proudly. I am a big believer in the Second Amendment.

Speech in Ayrshire, Scotland, July 31, 2015

Millions and millions of women—cervical cancer, breast cancer—are helped by Planned Parenthood. So you can say whatever you want, but they have millions of women going through Planned Parenthood that are helped greatly.

Republican presidential debate in Houston, Texas, February 25, 2016

But Planned Parenthood should absolutely be defunded. I mean, if you look at what's going on with that, it's terrible.

Interview with *Fox News Sunday*,
October 18, 2015

*I've made a lot of money with China, but you know what, they know. They told me. That's how they do it. **It's the single greatest tool they have, currency manipulation, and they're grand masters.** They do a great job. I congratulate them. I'm not angry at China. I'm angry at our country for allowing them to do it.*

Campaign rally,
St. Augustine, Florida, October 24, 2016

Why would I call China a currency manipulator when they are working with us on the North Korean problem? We will see what happens!

Twitter, April 16, 2017

I see NATO as a good thing.

Interview with *The Washington Post*,
March 21, 2016

I think NATO is obsolete.

Interview with *ABC News*,
March 27, 2016

THEY ARE THE MOST DISHONEST PEOPLE IN THE WORLD. THE MEDIA. THEY ARE THE WORST. THEY ARE THE WORST. THEY ARE VERY DISHONEST PEOPLE.

Campaign rally in Indianapolis,
Indiana, April 20, 2016

OK, NO, I DON'T HATE ANYBODY.
I LOVE THE MEDIA. THEY'RE
WONDERFUL, I GUESS WE
WOULDN'T BE HERE, MAYBE,
IF IT WASN'T FOR THE MEDIA,
SO MAYBE WE SHOULDN'T BE
COMPLAINING.

Campaign rally in
Indianapolis, Indiana,
April 20, 2016

Well, I read a lot . . .
and over my life,
I've read so much.

Interview with *The Hugh Hewitt Show*, February 25, 2015

I don't read much.
Mostly I read contracts,
but usually my lawyers
do most of the work.
There are too many pages.

Interview with *Veja*, February 18, 2014

I don't have a lot of time for listening to television.

In court proceedings documented by *The New York Times*, July 28, 2015

I actually love watching television.

Interview with *The Hugh Hewitt Show*, February 25, 2015

I DON'T WANT TO BE PROVOCATIVE, AND IN MANY CASES I TRY NOT TO BE PROVOCATIVE.

Time to Get Tough: Making America #1 Again, 2011

I DO LOVE PROVOKING PEOPLE. THERE IS TRUTH TO THAT.

Interview with *Buzzfeed*,
February 13, 2014

Sometimes, part of making a deal is denigrating your competition.

Trump: The Art of the Deal, 1987

If striving for wholeness means diminishing your competition, then your competition wasn't much to begin with.

Trump: Think Like a Champion, 2009

You've gotta be nice.

Interview with *The New Yorker*,
May 19, 1997

I do believe in hate when it's appropriate.

Trump: Surviving at the Top, 1990

I avoid people
with especially
high opinions of
their own abilities
or worth.

Trump: Think Big, 2007

Hey, look, I went to the hardest school to get into, the best school in the world, I guess you could say, the Wharton School of Finance. It's like super genius stuff.

Interview with CNN, August 11, 2015

Remember that in the best negotiations, everyone wins.

Trump: Never Give Up, 2008

You hear lots of people say that a great deal is when both sides win. That is a bunch of crap.

Trump: Think Big, 2007

I think there are two Donald Trumps.

News conference,
Palm Beach, Florida,
March 11, 2016

I don't think there are two Donald Trumps. I think there's one Donald Trump.

News conference,
Palm Beach, Florida,
March 11, 2016

Eminent domain is wonderful.

Interview with *Fox News*,
October 6, 2015

I don't like eminent domain.

Interview with *Breitbart News*,
November 5, 2015

I'm an environmentalist.

Interview with *Larry King Live*, CNN,
April 28, 2010

Global warming is a total, and very expensive, hoax!

Twitter, December 6, 2013

THE ELECTORAL COLLEGE IS A DISASTER FOR A DEMOCRACY.

Twitter, November 6, 2012

WITCH
HUNT

I am an innocent man being persecuted by some very bad, conflicted & corrupt people in a Witch Hunt that is illegal & should never have been allowed to start—And only because I won the Election! Despite this, great success!

Twitter, March 3, 2019

DOJ just issued the McCabe report—which is a total disaster. **He LIED! LIED! LIED!** McCabe was totally controlled by Comey— McCabe is Comey!! **NO COLLUSION, ALL MADE UP BY THIS DEN OF THIEVES AND LOWLIFES!**

Twitter, April 13, 2018

...MUELLER WAS NOT FIRED
AND WAS RESPECTFULLY
ALLOWED TO FINISH HIS WORK
ON WHAT I, AND MANY OTHERS,
SAY WAS AN ILLEGAL
INVESTIGATION (THERE WAS NO
CRIME), HEADED BY A TRUMP
HATER WHO WAS HIGHLY
CONFLICTED, AND A GROUP OF
18 VERY ANGRY DEMOCRATS.
DRAIN THE SWAMP!

Twitter, April 25, 2019

...Despite the fact that the Mueller Report was "composed" by Trump Haters and Angry Democrats, who had unlimited funds and human resources, the end result was No Collusion, No Obstruction. Amazing!

Twitter, April 25, 2019

I have been the most transparent president and administration in the history of our country by far.

To reporters outside
the White House,
April 24, 2019

Collusion is not a crime, but that doesn't matter because there was No Collusion (except by Crooked Hillary and the Democrats)!

Twitter, July 31, 2018

You know they have a
word, it sort of became
old-fashioned, it's called
a nationalist.
And I say, "really, we're not
supposed to use that word?"
Do you know what I am?
I'm a nationalist.

Campaign rally for Ted Cruz,
Houston, Texas,
October 22, 2019

My whole life has been heat. I like heat, in a certain way.

Immigration talk-a-thon,
January 9, 2018

PRESIDENTIAL HARASSMENT!

Twitter, April 18, 2019

No collusion.
No obstruction.
For the haters and
the radical left
democrats—
Game Over.

Twitter meme with
Game of Thrones imagery,
April 18, 2019

SO, IT HAS NOW BEEN DETERMINED, BY 18 PEOPLE THAT TRULY HATE PRESIDENT TRUMP, THAT THERE WAS NO COLLUSION WITH RUSSIA. IN FACT, IT WAS AN ILLEGAL INVESTIGATION THAT SHOULD NEVER HAVE BEEN ALLOWED TO START. I FOUGHT BACK HARD AGAINST THIS PHONY & TREASONOUS HOAX!

Twitter, April 10, 2019

What the Democrats have done in trying to steal a Presidential Election, first at the "ballot box" and then, after that failed, with the "Insurance Policy," is the biggest Scandal in the history of our Country!

Twitter, March 17, 2019

"Donald Trump was being framed, he fought back. That is not Obstruction." @JesseBWatters I had the right to end the whole Witch Hunt if I wanted. **I could have fired everyone,** including Mueller, if I wanted. I chose not to. I had the **RIGHT** to use **Executive Privilege.** I didn't!

Twitter, April 18, 2019

WITCH HUNT!

Twitter, February 27, 2018

What about these notes? Why do you take notes? Lawyers don't take notes. I never had a lawyer who took notes.

Speaking to Former White House Counsel Don McGahn, Mueller Report, February 26, 2018

I have no relationship with him other than he called me a genius. He said Donald Trump is a genius and he is going to be the leader of the party and he's going to be the leader of the world or something.

Campaign rally, in reference to Russian president Vladimir Putin, February 17, 2016

Oh my God. This is terrible.

In response to the appointment of Special Counsel for the Russia investigation, Mueller Report, March 17, 2017